CONTENTS

1.   Performance Test Definition

2.   Performance Test Objective

2.1. Performance Testing During Development

2.1.1 Using Continuous Integration to Detect Performance Degradation

2.2 Integration Performance Testing

2.3. Scalability Acceptance Testing

2.4. Platform Scalability Testing

3. Performance Test Types

3.1. User UI and/or Message API Simulations

3.1.1. Load Testing

3.1.2. Stress Testing

3.1.3. Soak Testing

3.1.4. Spike Testing

3.2. Batch Testing

3.3. Configuration / Proof of Concept Testing

3.4. Baselines

3.5. Benchmark

4. The Relationship between Performance Testing and Tuning

4.1. Cooperative Effort

4.2. Tuning Process Overview

5. Performance Testing Activities

5.1. NFRs, Volumetric Analysis and Test Planning

5.1.1. Activity 1. NFR Analysis

5.1.2. Activity 2. Identify Performance Acceptance Criteria

5.1.2. Activity 3. Volumetric Model Analysis

5.1.3. Activity 4. Performance Test Planning

5.2. Preparation and Setup

5.2.1. Activity 5. Obtain Test Environment

5.2.2. Activity 6. Configure the Test Environment

5.2.3. Activity 7. Create Scripts and Scenarios

5.2.4. Activity 8. Test Readiness Review (TRR)

5.3. Test Execution

5.3.1. Activity 9. Validate the Test Environment

5.3.2. Activity 10. Run the Performance Test Scenarios

5.4. Analyse Results and Report

5.4.1. Activity 11. Analyse Results

5.4.2. Activity 12. Test Completion Report

5.4.3. Activity 13. Revisit Activities and Consider Acceptance Criteria

5.4.4. Activity 14. Re-prioritise Tasks

6. Performance Test Tools

7. Diagnostics and Performance Monitoring

8. Test Data

9. Conclusion

10. Failure Modes Effects and Criticality Analysis (FMECA)

11. Introduction

12. Overview

13 Methodology

13.1. Steps

13.2. Risk Evaluation

14. Using FMECA

  13.1. When to do a FMECA

  14.2. Types of FMECA

    14.2.1. Hardware

    14.2.2. Software

    14.2.3. System

15. Conclusion

Appendix A – Example FMECA Worksheet

Appendix B – Example Rating Scores

Appendix C – Example Risk Matrix

1. PERFORMANCE TEST DEFINITION

In quality assurance, performance testing is a practice aimed at evaluating how a system performs in terms of responsiveness and stability under specific workloads. It can also be used to assess, measure, validate, or verify other quality attributes of a service or application, such as scalability, availability, reliability, and resource utilization.

2. PERFORMANCE TEST OBJECTIVE

Performance testing plays a crucial role in the Software Development Life Cycle (SDLC), whether following the Waterfall or Agile methodologies. From the initial planning phase to production or live deployment, it steers the development process toward delivering higher-quality software. Stakeholders, designers, developers, subject matter experts (SMEs), and testers should prioritize performance considerations throughout every stage of the SDLCâ€"from initiation and development to production and live operation. The figure below illustrates where performance testing fits within the SDLC.

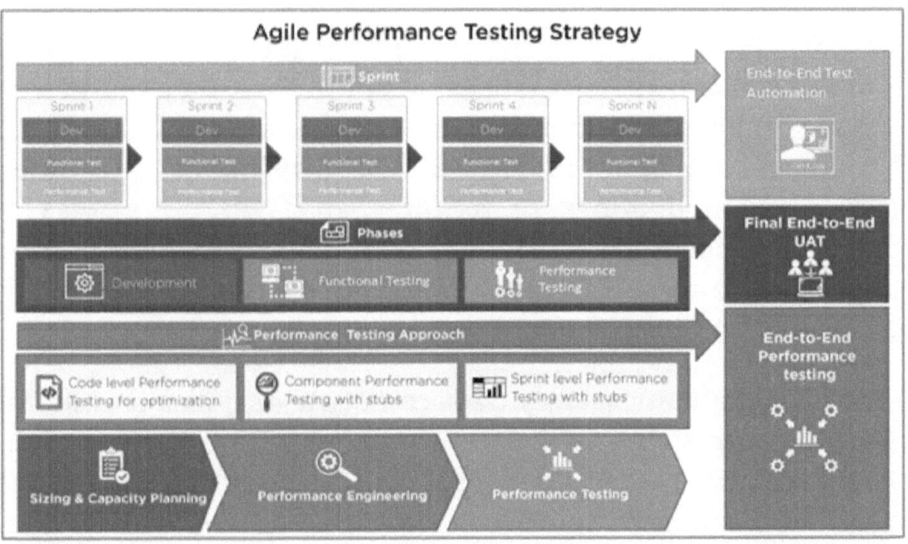

[1] The term SDLC throughout this course refers to both Waterfall and Agile developments. [2] The term stakeholder is used to refer to any person or group who will be affected by the system directly or indirectly

2.1. Performance Testing During Development

Performance testing should begin during the development phase within the Agile squad, focusing on both code and component levels.

Agile Performance Testing

The primary objective of Agile performance testing is to evaluate the performance of critical business processes as early as possible within each sprint test cycle. This involves identifying, isolating, and resolving performance bottlenecks stemming from design flaws or issues at the code, microservice, component or with the complete inegreated system.

The Agile squad should focus on performance testing the most significant or critical user journeys within their services, guided by agreed-upon Non-Functional Requirements (NFRs). These tests should be automated as part of the continuous integration process and maintained to reflect changes in the service or application functionality. The primary focus of these tests is on latency and transaction capabilities, aligning with the specific objectives of the testing phase.

During development sprints, performance tests typically simulate individual users or small user groups/messages based on the system resources available. Consequently, these tests are limited to load and soak testing using a fraction (e.g., 1/n) of the "Busy Hour" load, without stress testing. Comparative tests between builds or releases, such as measuring single-transaction latency, help identify opportunities for optimizing design or code.

The artifacts generated during the Development Performance Testing phase, such as tool-specific scripts and data creation, are reused in subsequent stages, including Integration and Scalability Testing. These artifacts assist in evaluating throughput against the NFRs linked to the User Stories.

Considerations for Development Environments

It is acknowledged that development environments often differ from production or live environments. Discrepancies in network, configuration, and infrastructure between the test and production environments must be carefully considered, as they may limit the scope and accuracy of performance testing.

2.1.1 Using Continuous Integration to Detect Performance Degradation

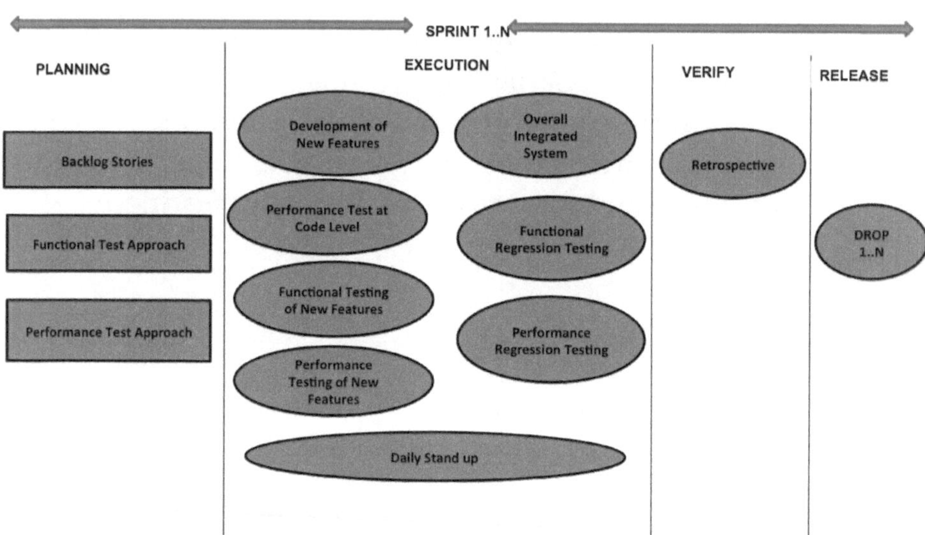

When conducting performance testing, the goal is typically to simulate the expected load in an environment closely resembling the Production/Live environment. Integrating performance testing into the Continuous Integration (CI) process enables early detection of performance degradations during development. This is achieved by running daily or weekly "small test cases" with relatively light loads, combined with strong assertions.

The objective is to measure the impact of newly committed code on the performance of microservices, individual services, or integrated systems. If a negative impact is detected, testers and developers can promptly assess and address the issue before advancing the changes to the next stage of the development lifecycle.

As with any CI test automation process, these smaller performance tests should be executed for every build or release by each Agile sprint. If running these tests becomes too time-intensive, they can be time-boxed, scheduled at agreed intervals, or conducted as part of a separate sprint. Performance test scripts must include precise assertions to generate alerts if performance degrades.

Assertions should be aligned with business requirements to define acceptable performance thresholds. To ensure this approach's effectiveness, testers should consider the following key points:

Environment Exclusiveness: Performance testing requires an exclusive environment to ensure results are solely due to the performance test, not influenced by other services.

Types of Scenarios to Run: Load Testing, Soak Testing

Metrics to Measure/Collect: Errors, Error Rate, Latency, Requests per Second (RPS)

Error Rate Threshold: Acceptable error rate is less than 1%. Determine how many users can receive an error message.

Response Time Metrics: 95th Percentile of response times should be less than the response times when the system breaks plus 10%.

User Tolerance for Response Times: Assess if a 5% worse response time for users is acceptable.

Requests per Second (RPS) Threshold: RPS should be greater than the requests per second when the system breaks minus 10%.

The margin of 10% mentioned in the last two points serves as a recommendation and can be adjusted according to the specific requirements defined for the project. It is crucial to understand that even when running the same test twice under identical conditions, the results will not be exactly the same. If the margin is set too small, tests may fail frequently due to false positives, indicating issues even when there is no actual degradation. On the other hand, if the margin is too large, there is a risk of missing real degradations, leading to false negatives. Therefore, a margin between 10% and 20% is generally considered a reasonable range to balance these concerns effectively.

In this approach, having a test environment that is smaller than the production environment is advantageous, as it simplifies the process of identifying the breaking point of the microservices, services, or integrated system being tested. Multiple test cycles may be required to accurately determine the system's breakpoint. During each test run, the tester should monitor how requests per second (RPS) increase in alignment with the number of users. If the tester observes that RPS remains unchanged or decreases, it indicates that some component is saturated and that the system is no longer able to scale, thereby revealing the breakpoint.

Once the assertions and scenarios are established, it is essential for the tester to review the tests in subsequent cycles to ensure stability and identify any necessary adjustments. Continuous Integration (CI) implies that test results must be monitored consistently, including regular reviews of assertions.

The benefits of this approach mirror those associated with CI/CD practices: rapid feedback, increased confidence in each build, and enhanced understanding of factors that cause failures in microservices or integrated services, which can help prevent similar errors in other areas of the application.

Moreover, early performance checks allow for robust code and functionality to be delivered before product release. By addressing performance early in the software development lifecycle, this approach can lead to significant cost savings by avoiding expensive code or software changes later on. Additionally, conducting performance testing in parallel with software development within sprints can reduce time to release compared to more traditional methods like waterfall or sprint hardening.

This approach focuses on three key areas:

1. Performance or response time testing at the code level
2. Performance or response time testing for newly developed features
3. Performance regression testing for the overall system integrated with these new features.

2.2 Integration Performance Testing

Integration Performance Testing involves combining individual microservices, components and products to evaluate their performance as a cohesive system. The primary goal of this testing level is to identify performance issues that may arise from the interactions between the integrated microservices, components and products.

To facilitate Integration Performance Testing, test drivers and stubs are commonly employed, and this testing is typically conducted within an integration sprint.

2.3. Scalability Acceptance Testing

Scalability Acceptance Testing (SAT) is a critical process designed to verify that the overall system performs as required under realistic loads and volumes. During SAT, the "Service" is evaluated against predefined Non-Functional Requirements (NFRs) and Service Level Agreements (SLAs), which typically encompass metrics such as the number of concurrent users, response times, requests, message or transaction throughput.

The primary objective of SAT is to determine the performance characteristics of a "Service" in a production or live environment.

To achieve this, the test environment must be an exact replica of the production or live environment. However, it differs in one crucial aspect: the addition of load-generation and resource-monitoring tools. These tools are essential for simulating realistic user loads and accurately measuring system performance under various conditions.

By conducting SAT, organizations can gain confidence in their system's ability to handle the expected number of users, workloads and identify potential bottlenecks or performance issues before deployment to the live environment. This proactive approach helps ensure a smooth transition to production and minimizes the risk of performance-related problems affecting end-users.

2.4. Platform Scalability Testing

To ensure that any proposed new platform can meet the needs of all services, Platform Scalability Testing (PST) is essential. This process verifies that the overall platform performs as required under specified load conditions, as defined by the Non-Functional Requirements (NFRs) and Service Level Agreements (SLAs) related to the number of services deployed on the platform.

The primary objective of PST is to assess the performance characteristics of the infrastructure. To achieve this, the testing environment must be an exact replica of the production infrastructure, enhanced with load-generation and resource-monitoring tools. These additions are crucial for simulating realistic load conditions and accurately evaluating how the platform will perform under various scenarios.

3. PERFORMANCE TEST TYPES

In software engineering, Performance Testing encompasses all subcategories of performance-related testing. Generally, the purpose of Performance Testing is to:

Assess Behavior: Evaluate the infrastructure, requests messaging, application, or service in terms of responsiveness, scalability, and stability under specific workload profiles.

Validate Compliance: Measure and validate performance against Service Level Agreements (SLAs) and Non-Functional Requirements (NFRs).

Collect Metrics: Gather metrics that enable stakeholders to make informed decisions regarding the overall quality of the infrastructure and application code being delivered. This data also helps estimate the hardware configuration necessary to support the application(s) in a production or live environment.

By conducting thorough Performance Testing, organizations can ensure that their systems meet both user expectations and operational requirements effectively.

Performance tests belong to one of the following types:

3.1. User UI and/or Message API Simulations

3.1.1. Load Testing

The diagram below depicts the typical profile of a Load Test. Initially, each functional area is tested individually under 'Peak / Busy Hour' load conditions. This is followed by a combined Load Test that also simulates 'Peak / Busy Hour' load across all areas

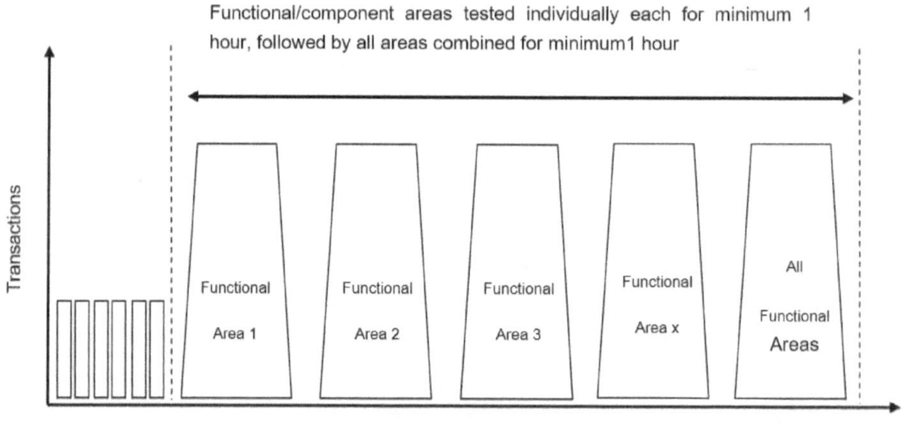

Load Tests are performed based on anticipated peak user activity, request, message throughput, and API interactions. The primary objective is to assess the response times for various time-sensitive requests, messages, transactions, or business processes to ensure they align with the documented Non-Functional Requirements (NFRs) and Service Level Agreements (SLAs). Additionally, the test evaluates the system's ability to operate correctly under load by measuring pass rates, failure rates, and error rates.

3.1.2. Stress Testing

The diagram below provides an overview of a typical Stress Test profile. This test is designed to identify scalability limitations by gradually increasing the throughput rate until a significant bottleneck or constraint in the system is detected. It helps to pinpoint where performance begins to degrade beyond acceptable limits and identifies which components of the system become constrained.

To prevent initialization and startup delays from skewing the test results—such as those related to resource pools and memory structures for Linux, Windows, and database servers—all simulated transactions are activated during a warm-up period before subjecting the system to higher loads.

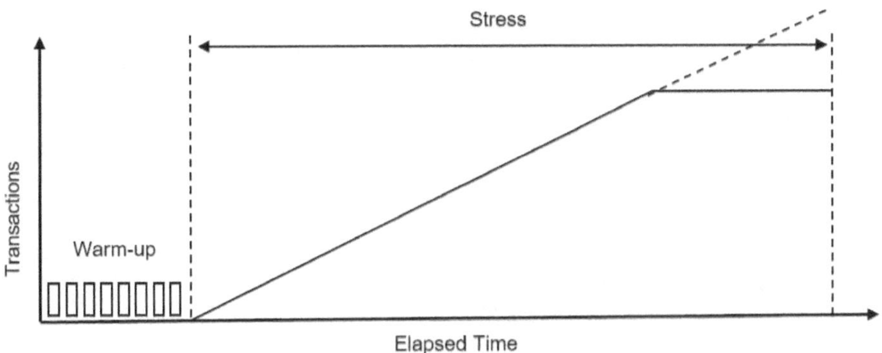

3.1.3. Soak Testing

The diagram below illustrates a typical Soak Test profile, which is conducted over an extended period—ideally simulating a week's worth of activity. This test aims to identify stability limitations and detect any performance degradation that may occur over time, such as CPU creep, memory leaks, connection handle leaks, thread lockups, and the filling up of disk/file/log systems.

It is recommended that the soak test run for a minimum of 48 hours, with an ideal duration of five days. To prevent initialization and startup delays from skewing the test results—such as those related to resource pools and memory structures for Linux, Windows, and database servers—all simulated transactions will be activated during a warm-up period before applying higher loads at the start of the test.

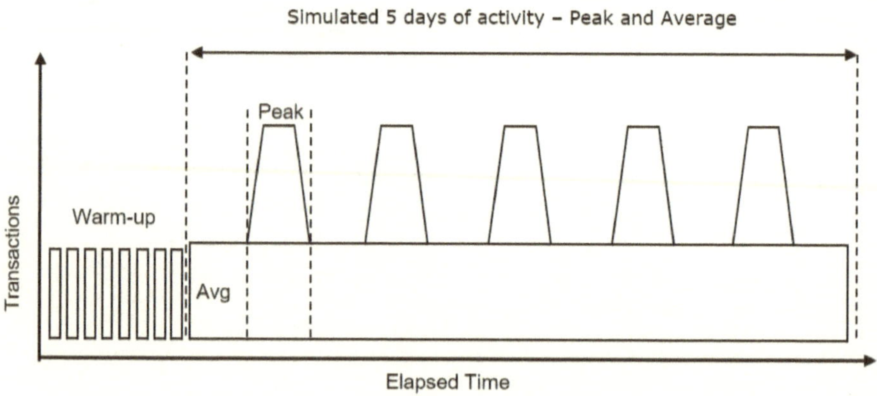

3.1.4. Spike Testing

The diagram below provides an overview of a typical Spike Test profile. The goal of this type of performance test is to assess the stability of the system during unpredictable bursts of high activity over varying time periods. This testing helps determine how well the system recovers between these sudden spikes in activity.

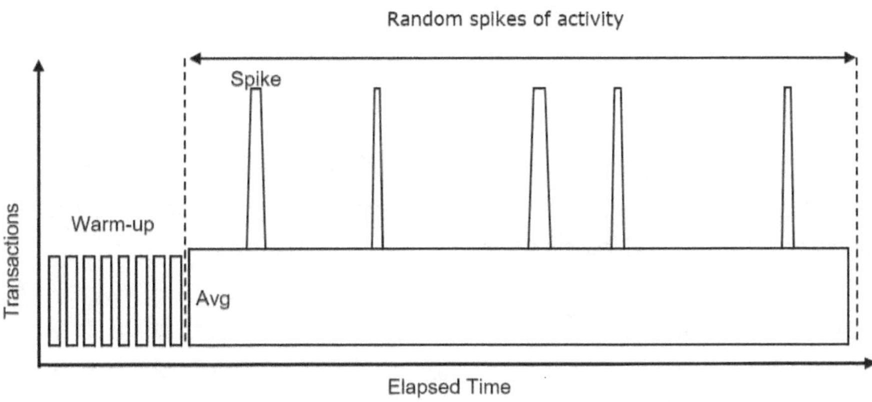

3.2. Batch Testing

A batch job is a scheduled program that operates without user intervention. The objectives of batch performance testing include ensuring that, regardless of data volume, the batch process performs efficiently enough to complete within the constraints of system resources and the designated time frame to meet Service Level Agreements (SLAs). Ideally, the execution of a batch job should not negatively impact the performance of other processes running on the system.

3.3. Configuration / Proof of Concept Testing

Instead of focusing on performance from a load perspective, tests are designed to assess the performance impact of configuration changes made to the components of the system.

A common example of this would be experimenting with various load-balancing or storage methods. This type of testing is often referred to as "Proof of Concept (PoC)" Testing.

3.4. Baselines

Creating a baseline involves conducting tests to capture performance metrics, which are essential for evaluating the effectiveness of subsequent performance improvements made to the system. By comparing future performance against this baseline, it becomes possible to determine whether performance is improving or degrading, as well as to identify deviations across different builds and versions.

Key considerations for establishing a baseline include:

Scope: A baseline can be created for an entire system, a batch job, an application, a microservice, a service, or a specific component.

Standard for Comparison: The baseline serves as a standard for comparison and helps track future optimizations. Therefore, it is crucial to ensure that the baseline results are repeatable.

Performance Changes: Baselines help identify changes in performance that indicate either degradation or optimization throughout the Development Life Cycle, as well as estimate "go live" behavior.

Reusability: Baseline assets should be reusable for future testing and evaluations.

Metrics: Baselines consist of various metrics that can be articulated through a broad set of key performance indicators, including response time, processor capacity, memory usage, disk capacity, and network bandwidth.

Shared Reference: Baselines provide a shared frame of reference. Sharing baseline results fosters a common understanding of the performance characteristics of the system.

Understanding System Behavior: It is essential to have a complete understanding of the system's behavior at the time the baseline is established. Failing to do so before implementing changes can be counterproductive.

Note: Baselines are not static; they evolve over time. Periodic redefinition of the baseline may be necessary due to changes implemented since the baseline was first established. If a project involves significant re-engineering of the system, it is essential to establish a new baseline.

3.5. Benchmark

In computing, a benchmark refers to the process of executing a computer program, a set of programs, or other operations to evaluate the relative performance of a target system. This is typically done by conducting a series of standard tests and trials. Consequently, benchmarking involves comparing the system's performance against an established standard baseline.

4. THE RELATIONSHIP BETWEEN PERFORMANCE TESTING AND TUNING

When performance testing uncovers characteristics that are considered unacceptable, the emphasis should transition from performance testing to performance tuning.

This shift aims to identify ways to enhance the system's performance to acceptable levels.

4.1. Cooperative Effort

Tuning is not typically the direct responsibility of performance testers; It is most effective when it involves collaboration among all stakeholders associated with the infrastructure, middleware, messaging, or services being tested.

This includes product vendors, architects, developers, testers, database administrators, system administrators, and network administrators.

Without the cooperation of a cross-functional team, achieving the system-wide perspective needed to effectively and efficiently resolve performance issues becomes nearly impossible. Tuning often requires additional tests, monitoring of components, resources, measuring response times under various load conditions and configurations.

4.2. Tuning Process Overview

Tuning follows an iterative process that is typically separate from, yet closely related to, the performance testing approach. Here's a brief overview of a typical tuning process:

When tests reveal unacceptable performance characteristics, the performance testing and tuning teams enter a diagnostic and remediation phase, involving multiple cycles of testing and tuning that require changes to be applied to the system.

Temporary modifications may be implemented intentionally to amplify an issue for diagnostic purposes or to assess whether specific changes can lead to improved performance.

It is essential that tests are conducted within a well-defined, controlled test environment to ensure that the configuration and initial test results are known and reproducible.

The performance testing and tuning teams should have full and exclusive control over this test environment to maximize the effectiveness of the tuning phase.

After each individual change is made to the system under test, tests should be executed or re-executed to measure the effectiveness of those changes.

The tuning process involves a rapid sequence of changes and tests. If a cooperative performance testing and tuning team is not fully available and dedicated during this phase, the process can take significantly longer.

Once the tuning phase is complete, the test environment is typically reset to its initial state. Successful remedial changes are reapplied, while any unsuccessful changes, along with temporary instrumentation and diagnostic modifications, are discarded.

The performance test should then be repeated to verify that the correct changes have been implemented. Additionally, the test environment may be adjusted to reflect new expectations regarding the minimum requirements for the production environment.

After completing the test and tune cycle, a new baseline must be established.

5. PERFORMANCE TESTING ACTIVITIES

There are six major stages that require careful planning:

1. Non-Functional Requirements (NFRs), Volumetric Model Analysis and Test Planning

2. Preparation and Setup

3. Informal Test Execution

4. Test Readiness Review (TRR), which may include defining what "DONE" means at the Agile Squad level for a User Story related to performance.

5. Formal Test Execution and Results Analysis

6. Test Completion Report

The following sections provide more detailed insights into these steps, while the flow diagrams below offer a breakdown at a more granular level

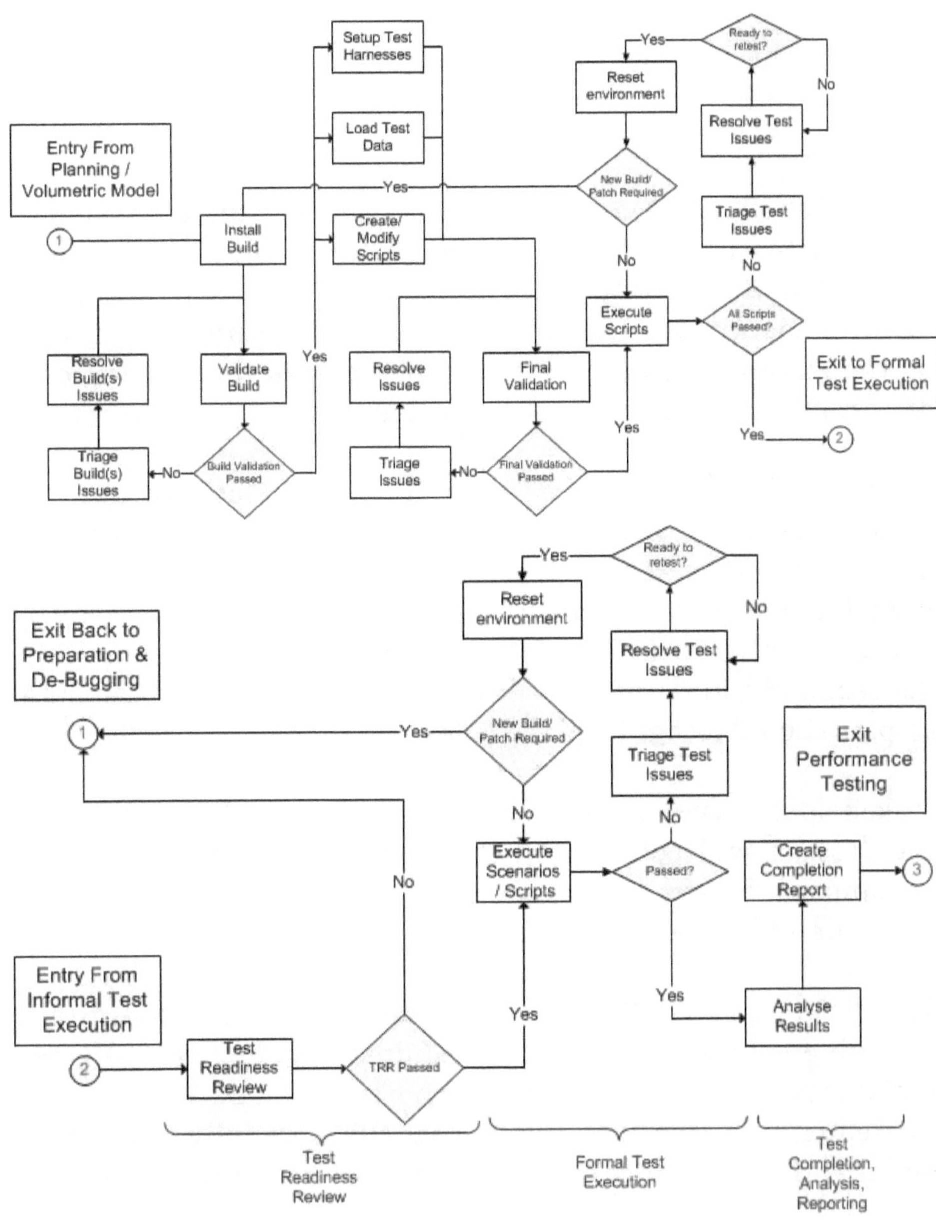

Entry From Planning / Volumetric Model
1
Install Build
Setup Test Harnesses
Load Test Data
Create/ Modify Scripts
Yes
Resolve Build(s) Issues
Validate Build
Yes
Triage Build(s) Issues
No
Build Validation Passed
Resolve Issues
Final Validation
Triage Issues
No
Final Validation Passed
Yes
Execute Scripts
New Build/ Patch Required
No
Reset environment
Yes
Ready to retest?
No
Resolve Test Issues
Triage Test Issues
No
All Scripts Passed?
Yes
Exit to Formal Test Execution
2
Exit Back to Preparation & De-Bugging
1
Yes
New Build/ Patch Required
No
Reset environment
Yes
Ready to retest?
No
Resolve Test Issues
Triage Test Issues
No
Execute Scenarios / Scripts
Passed?
Yes
Exit Performance Testing
Create Completion Report
3
Analyse Results
Yes
Entry From Informal Test Execution
2
Test Readiness Review
No
TRR Passed
Yes
Test Readiness Review
Formal Test Execution
Test Completion, Analysis, Reporting

5.1. NFRs, Volumetric Analysis and Test Planning

5.1.1. Activity 1. NFR Analysis

A Non-Functional Requirement (NFR) outlines the criteria used to evaluate the operation of the Platform and its Products, rather than detailing specific functional behaviors. NFR analysis involves identifying the descriptions of the services provided by the Platform and each Product, along with their operational constraints and Service Level Agreements (SLAs).

NFRs should be differentiated between the Platform and the Products deployed on it. Each Change and/or Squad will effectively inherit the NFRs, Operational Level Agreements (OLAs), and SLAs for their Product, making it essential for them to actively assess whether planned changes will affect those baselines. Consequently, identifying stakeholders should be a fundamental step, as should recognizing the NFRs.

Stakeholders have implicit expectations regarding how well the Product will perform on the Platform. These expectations encompass factors such as execution speed, reliability, and behavior under unexpected conditions.

The NFRs must define these characteristics of the system, including volumetrics, the time required to complete tasks, and the number of concurrent users supported.
Therefore, it is crucial to ensure that NFRs are fully understood and that the acceptance criteria for the system are clearly defined.

Steps for Stakeholder and Goal Analysis

Identify Key Stakeholders:
Begin by identifying the primary stakeholders associated with both 'the Platform' and 'the Product'.

Generate Goals from Stakeholders:
Based on the knowledge and experience of the stakeholders, articulate their goals.

Decompose Goals into Sub-goals:
Break down each identified goal into smaller, more manageable sub-goals.

Identify Non-Functional Requirements (NFRs):
For each sub-goal, determine the non-functional requirements that must be met.

Rules for the Process

Who: Identify the stakeholders involved.

What: Define the services or goals to be achieved.

How: Determine how the sub-goals will be accomplished within given constraints.

The above five rules can be visualised in the following story.

"Who; is the stakeholder; What; are the services (goals) that the system should provide to the stakeholder, What; are the sub goals, How; does the system perform under the sub goals constraints"

Checklist for Validating Non-Functional Requirements (NFRs)

Source Verification: Does each requirement have a clearly defined source?

Achievability in Test Environment: Is each requirement feasible within the available test environment?

Testability Post-Implementation: Can each requirement be tested once it is implemented?

Clarity and Boundaries: Is each requirement clearly defined and unambiguous?

Conflict Assessment: Do any requirements conflict with one another?

Traceability to System Goals: Is each requirement traceable back to the system's goals?

Quantitative Boundaries: Is each requirement expressed in quantitative terms?
Clarity of Expression: Are the requirements stated clearly, and is there potential for misinterpretation?

5.1.2. Activity 2. Identify Performance Acceptance Criteria

Ideally, the process of identifying or estimating the desired performance characteristics of the Platform and its Products should begin early in the System Development Life Cycle (SDLC). This involves documenting the performance attributes that users and stakeholders associate with good performance.

Characteristics that typically correlate with user or stakeholder satisfaction include:

Response Time: For instance, a specified percentage (e.g., 90%) of response times for message/transaction <x> must be under <n> seconds. It's important to note that response times generally follow a statistical distribution, and certain common measures can have drawbacks. For example, using the average means that 50% of values will exceed the requirement by definition, while setting a maximum allows for one outlier to cause a failure to meet the requirement. A practical approach is to specify that the response time should not be exceeded by 90% of values. Additionally, it may be beneficial to categorize response time targets by transaction type (e.g., Read, Write, Update) to better reflect the user experience while accommodating a small number of outliers. This categorization is also supported by most testing tools.

Batch Elapsed Time: For example, batch job <MY-BATCH-JOB> must start by hh:mm and complete processing by hh:mm.

Throughput: For instance, the Platform and/or Product must support <n> messages per second.

Resource Utilization: For example, Platform processor utilization should not exceed <p>%. Other critical resources to consider when setting objectives include memory, disk input/output (I/O), network I/O, and latency.

5.1.3. Activity 3. Volumetric Model Analysis

In the context of Performance Testing, Volumetric Model analysis is an analytical approach used to determine the expected load during peak business periods. The figure below illustrates the Volumetric Model Life Cycle:

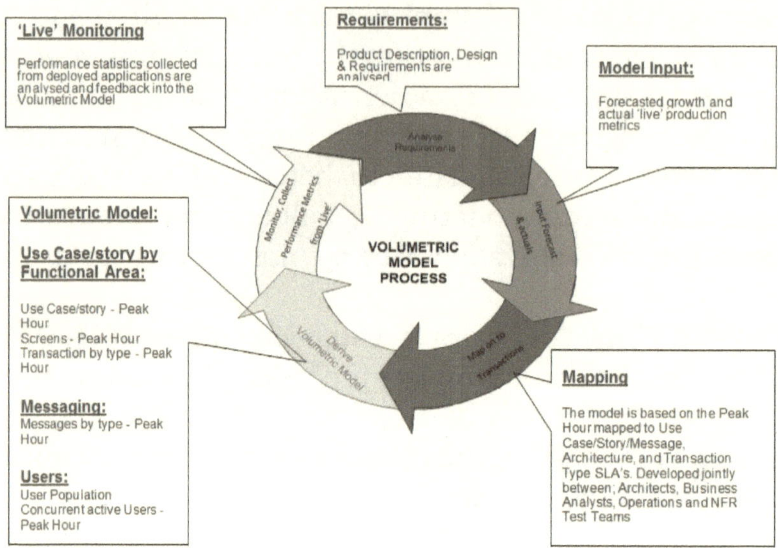

The flow diagram below outlines the process for the Volumetric Model that should be followed:

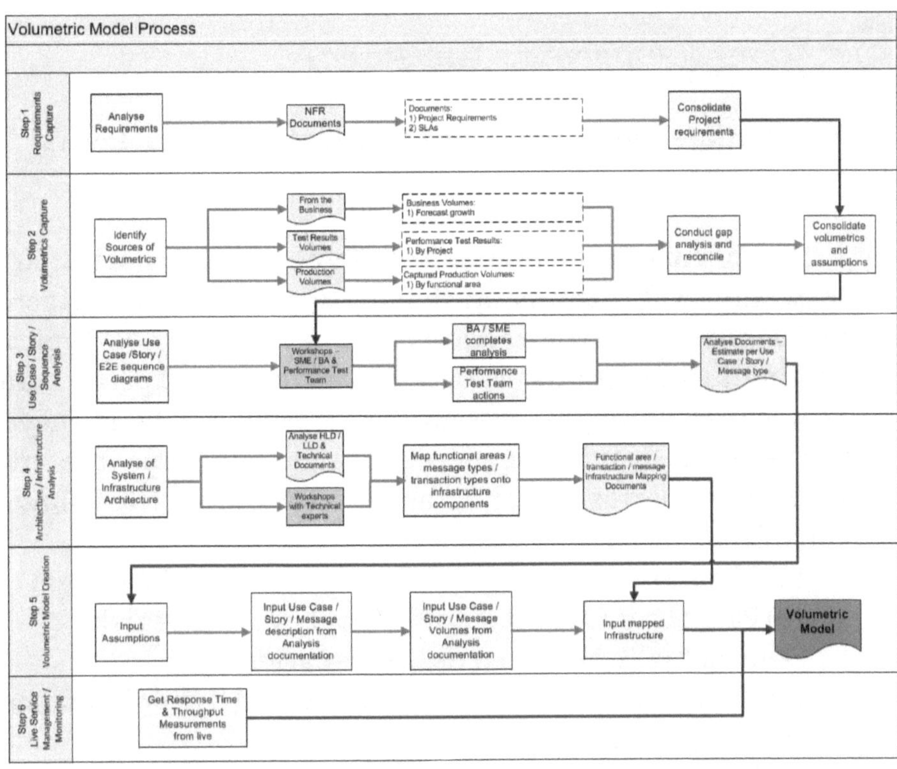

Volumetric Model Process
Step 1 Requirements Capture
Analyse Requirements
NFR Documents
Documents:
1) Project Requirements
2) SLAs
Consolidate Project requirements
Step 2 Volumetrics Capture
Identify Sources of Volumetrics
From the Business
Business Volumes:
1) Forecast growth
Test Results Volumes
Performance Test Results:
1) By Project
Production Volumes
Captured Production Volumes:
1) By functional area
Conduct gap analysis and reconcile
Consolidate volumetrics and assumptions
Step 3 Use Case / Story / Sequence Analysis
Analyse Use Case /Story / E2E sequence diagrams
Workshops – SME / BA & Performance Test Team
BA / SME completes analysis
Performance Test Team actions
Analyse Documents – Estimate per Use Case / Story / Message type
Step 4 Architecture / Infrastructure Analysis
Analyse of System / Infrastructure Architecture
Analyse HLD / LLD & Technical Documents
Workshops with Technical experts
Map functional areas / message types / transaction types onto infrastructure components
Functional area / transaction / message Infrastructure Mapping Documents
Step 5 Volumetric Model Creation
Input Assumptions
Input Use Case / Story / Message description from Analysis documentation
Input Use Case / Story / Message Volumes from Analysis documentation
Input mapped Infrastructure
Volumetric Model
Step 6 Live Service Management / Monitoring
Get Response Time & Throughput Measurements from live

5.1.4. Activity 4. Performance Test Planning

Planning and scripting performance tests involves several key steps:

1. **Identifying Performance Test Types and Scenarios:** Refer to Section 3 for details on the appropriate variability across users, messages, transactions, etc. Key scenarios typically emerge during the process of defining the desired performance characteristics of the system (see Section 5.1.1). If they do not emerge, it will be necessary to determine the most valuable scenarios to script, taking into account the following considerations:
    (a) The most frequently used paths through the system
    (b) Paths that present significant performance risks
    Contractually obligated usage scenarios
    (c) Usage scenarios implied or mandated by performance testing goals and objectives
    (d) The most common usage scenarios
    (e) Business-critical usage scenarios
    (f) Performance-intensive usage scenarios
    (g) Usage scenarios that raise technical concerns
    (h) Usage scenarios that are of concern to stakeholders

2. **Identifying Required Test Scripts.**

3. **Identifying UI, API and Batch Processes.**

4. **Identifying Test Data Requirements.**

5. **Identifying Test Environment Requirements.**

6. **Identifying Performance Metrics to be Captured.**

7. **Identifying Resource and Support Requirements.**

5.2. Preparation and Setup

5.2.1. Activity 5. Obtain Test Environment

The environment in which performance tests are conducted, along with the tools and necessary hardware, constitutes the Performance Test Environment/Service, which must be capable of executing performance tests. If the objective is to determine the performance characteristics of the system in a production setting, the test environment should closely replicate the production environment, supplemented by load-generation and resource-monitoring tools.

However, exact replicas of test environments are rare; therefore, the degree of similarity between the hardware, software, and network configurations of the system under test and those in actual production is a critical factor when selecting performance tests and applicable loads. It is important to recognize that both the physical and software environments affect performance testing, as well as the specific objectives of the test.

A key factor in identifying the appropriate test environment is to thoroughly understand the similarities and differences between the test and production environments.

Some critical factors to consider are:

Hardware Configurations:

Machine Hardware: Specifications for processor and memory.

Virtualization: Use of shared hardware across different environments.

Network: Network architecture and locations of end users/endpoints. Implications for load balancing. Configurations for clusters and Domain Name System (DNS). Shared networks with other environments.

Tools:

Load-Generation Tool Limitations: Constraints associated with load-generation tools.

Environmental Impact of Monitoring Tools: Effects of monitoring tools on the environment.

Software:

Installed Software: Other software present in or shared within virtual environments.

Software License Constraints: Variations or restrictions in software licenses.

Storage Capacity and Seed Data Volume: Considerations for storage limits and initial data volumes.

Logging Levels: Specifications for logging levels used.

External Factors:

Network Traffic: Volume and type of additional traffic on the network.

Scheduled Processes: Impact of scheduled or background batch processes, updates, or backups.

System Interactions: Interactions with other systems that may affect performance.

5.2.2. Activity 6. Configure the Test Environment

Prepare the tools and resources needed to execute the test approach as features and components become available.

This step should be initiated as early as possible to ensure that the performance test team has the necessary resources and support from the outset.

Set up the load-generation tools, data generation tools, monitoring tools, and the system under test, ensuring that the environment meets engineering requirements.

The coordination phase of this step typically involves requesting assistance from managers and administrators to acquire and configure equipment and other resources that are not directly under the control of the test team or performance testers.

Checklist:

Questions to Ask:

Test Environment Size: What is the size of the test environment, and how does it compare to the production environment?

Environment Sharing: Who else is using or sharing the environment? Is exclusive use of the environment required during the performance test?

Administration Responsibilities:
Who administers the performance-test environment?
Who manages the application under test?
Who oversees the load-generation tool?
Who configures and operates resource monitors for the

system under test?
Who administers the data-generation tool?

Permissions and Access:

Are special permissions needed before generating a specific volume of load?
Who has the authority to reset the system under test?

Coordination Needs:

What other components require special coordination?
What security or authentication considerations exist for simulating multiple users?
What coordination is necessary for using recording and/or monitoring software?
What batch jobs and job sets need to be set up?
Do any housekeeping jobs need to be temporarily suspended?

Value Provided:

Ensures that both the load-generation and test environments are ready when needed.
Guarantees that test data is prepared in advance.
Clarifies points of contact for performance-testing environment support for the entire team.
Ensures that performance testing support staff understand their responsibilities.

Tasks Accomplished:

Performance-test environment configured and ready for test scripting.
Load-generation environment set up and ready for testing.
Support responsibilities assigned.
Special permissions and timing for high-load tests determined.

Coordination Required With:

> System Administrators
> Network Support
> Database Administrators
> Development Team
> Managers of the above teams

5.2.3. Activity 7. Create Scripts and Scenarios

Creating an executable performance test is specific to the tools being used. Regardless of the tool, the process typically involves writing several individual scripts and then combining these scripts to form a comprehensive performance test scenario [See Section 3].

Scripting Development Process and Standards

It is essential to adhere to the scripting development process and standards, guided by the following general principles:

Consistency in Development Process: The scripting development process must be uniform for all performance tests.

Uniform File Structure: The performance testing scripting file structure should be consistent across all test environments.

Configuration and Version Control Compliance: All scripts and associated data must comply with configuration and version control standards.

Script Types: Scripts should be categorized into three types:

> Data Setup
> Component
> End-to-End (E2E)

Adherence to Standards:
Each script must adhere to the following standards:
Maintain a consistent style.
Follow established naming conventions.
Be easy to read and understand.
Include annotations and comments for clarity.
Be easily maintainable by other team members.

5.2.4. Activity 8. Test Readiness Review (TRR)

Performance testing tasks do not occur in isolation; therefore, the performance test specialist must collaborate with other teams to prioritize and coordinate support, resources, and schedules to ensure efficiency and success. It is advisable to conduct a Test Readiness Review (TRR) before test execution to assess whether the system under review is prepared to move into performance testing.

This involves determining if the test procedures are complete, verifying their compliance with test plans, dependencies, and entry criteria, and confirming that the agreed-upon definition of "DONE" has been met.

Note: The TRR may align with the definition of "DONE" at the Agile level for a User Story related to performance. The scope of the TRR is directly linked to the risk level associated with conducting the planned performance test and the significance of the test evaluation results for overall project or program success. The specific risk level will vary as the system progresses from development to production/live environments. Early development performance tests may not require the same level of review as final tests. Sound judgment should guide the scope of each specific test or series of tests.

Checklist:

Questions to Ask:

Test Objective: What is the objective of the planned test?

Scenario Confirmation: Which set of scenarios will be executed?

Requirement Verification: Does the planned test verify a requirement that is directly traceable to a system specification or other program requirements?

Scope of Testing: What is being tested (e.g., component, integration, system, system of systems, product, platform)?

Configuration Maturity: Is the configuration of the system under test sufficiently mature, defined, and representative to achieve the planned test objectives?

Preliminary Tests Completion: Have all planned preliminary tests—informal, functional, unit level, component, integration, system, performance tests, and qualification tests—been conducted with satisfactory results?

Resource Availability: Is the planned test adequately resourced in terms of personnel, test assets, facilities, data systems, support equipment, and logistics?

Testing Readiness: Are we ready to begin testing?

Risk Assessment: What are the risks associated with the tests, and how are they being mitigated?
Fallback Plan: What is the fallback plan if a technical issue or potential showstopper arises during testing?

Value Provided:
Assurance that previous component, subsystem, and system test results provide a satisfactory basis for proceeding with planned tests.
Identification of risk levels that are acceptable to project/ program leadership.

Tasks Accomplished:
Completion and approval of test plans for the system under test.
Identification and coordination of required test resources.
Fulfillment of test entry criteria.

Coordination Required With
Managers and stakeholders
Developers
System administrators
Database administrators
Test environment support
Users or user representatives

5.3. Test Execution

5.3.1. Activity 9. Validate the Test Environment

Before executing tests, it is crucial to validate that the test environment aligns with the expected or designed configuration for the type of performance test being conducted.

If the delivered test environment differs from the one for which the tests were designed, there is a significant risk that the tests may fail or, even worse, succeed while yielding misleading results.

Checklist:

TRR Completion: Has the Test Readiness Review (TRR) been conducted, and have the risks and issues raised during the TRR been mitigated or resolved?

Test Environment Validation: Validate that the test environment matches the configuration expected for the planned performance test scenario.

Performance Metrics Configuration: Ensure that the test environment is correctly configured to collect performance metrics.

Confidence Test Execution: Before running the formal test, conduct a quick "confidence" test to verify that the test scripts and remote performance counters are functioning correctly.

Workload Model Representation: Confirm that the execution of the test scenario accurately represents the workload model you intend to simulate.

System Reset: Reset the system before starting formal test execution, unless your scenario specifies otherwise.

Key Performance and Business Indicators: Ensure that the test is configured to collect key performance and business indicators of interest at this stage.

Validation of Assumptions and Techniques: Validate all test assumptions and techniques to ensure their appropriateness for the planned tests.

5.3.2. Activity 10. Run the Performance Test Scenarios

During the execution stage, the results of performance test scenarios and any defects are recorded to track and manage test progress until all planned tests are completed or the final acceptance milestone is achieved.

Performance testers execute the scenarios according to the test plan and report any performance issues to the relevant resolution team by raising a defect in the selected defect management tool. Additionally, appropriate performance monitoring tools are utilized to analyze and report on performance metrics

5.4. Analyse Results and Report

5.4.1. Activity 11. Analyse Results

Communicating Test Results and Insights

Managers and stakeholders require more than just test results; they need clear conclusions, consolidated data that supports those conclusions, and actionable recommendations. In contrast, technical team members seek detailed analyses, comparisons, and insights into how the results were obtained.

To enhance communication and collaboration:

Frequent Sharing of Results: Technical team members benefit from performance results being shared more frequently, ideally during test execution. Immediately share test results and make raw data accessible.

Collaborative Data Analysis: Analyze the data both individually and as part of a collaborative, cross-functional technical team.

Real-Time Performance Metrics Analysis: Monitor performance metrics in real time and compare the results against acceptable or expected levels to determine whether the system's performance is trending toward or away from its objectives.

Evaluate Preliminary Results: Assess whether the preliminary results are logical. If a test fails, a diagnosis and tuning activity are typically warranted. Once performance bottlenecks are addressed, repeat the test to validate the fixes.

Deep Analysis for Informed Decisions: Performance-testing results often allow for in-depth analysis of components, which can inform decisions about architecture design and business strategy.

Capture Additional Metrics: If the analysis does not fully explain the results of a particular test, additional metrics may need to be captured during subsequent test cycles.

Engage Subject Matter Experts: Consult with subject matter experts to confirm that the test achieved its intended outcomes and to clarify the significance of the captured performance metrics.

Modify Tests for Improved Insights: If the results do not align with the test's objectives, adjust the test to gather new, improved, or different information.

Set Priorities Based on Results: Use the test results to establish priorities for future tests.

Caution in Data Reduction: While collecting metrics can generate large volumes of data, be cautious when applying data-reduction techniques, as valuable information may be lost in the process.

5.4.2. Activity 12. Test Completion Report

Test Completion Reports are issued at the conclusion of each test cycle and provide a summary of the testing results, including any deviations from the scope outlined in the test plan.

Report Categories - Reports are categorized into two main types:

1. Technical Reports

Test Description: Provides a detailed overview of the test, including the workload model and test environment.

Data Presentation: Features easily digestible data with minimal pre-processing required.

Access to Information: Includes access to the complete data set, test conditions, and technical documentation.

Observations and Collaboration: Contains concise statements of observations, concerns, questions, and requests for collaboration.

2. Stakeholder Reports

Criteria Relevance: Outlines the criteria to which the results pertain.
Visual Data Representation: Offers intuitive, visual representations of the most relevant data.
Summary of Findings: Provides brief verbal summaries of charts or graphs in relation to the specified criteria.

Workload Model Visualization: Includes intuitive visual representations of the workload model and test environment.

Observations and Recommendations: Summarizes key observations, concerns, and actionable recommendations.

In most cases it is valuable to have a daily or every-other-day update to share information and co-ordinate next tasks.

5.4.3. Activity 13. Revisit Activities and Consider Acceptance Criteria

Between cycles, verify that the information remains unchanged. Incorporate any new information, such as customer or technical feedback, and update the performance tests as needed.

Checklist:

Questions to Ask:

Project Vision Changes: Have the performance implications of the project vision changed?

Service Performance Changes: Have the performance implications of the service being provided changed, or has the problem being addressed shifted?

Project Schedule and Resources: Have there been any changes to the project schedule, structure, or available resources?

Performance-Testing Objectives: Have the objectives for performance testing changed?

Validation of Performance Criteria: Do the performance-testing activities need to validate any changes in contractual, compliance, project, or customer performance criteria or expectations?

Addressing Performance Concerns: What performance-testing activities can help address currently known performance concerns?

Resource and Instrumentation Updates: Update assumptions regarding resources and instrumentation needs.

Identify Areas of Concern: Highlight any areas of concern related to performance.

Resource and Instrumentation Risks: Identify resource and instrumentation needs and potential risks.

Update Usage Scenarios: Enhance and update usage scenarios related to specific performance concerns.

Refine Performance Goals: Enhance and update performance goals, requirements, targets, and thresholds.

Team Communication on Testing Activities: Ensure that the team receives adequate notice about upcoming performance-testing activities that will require additional support from team members.

Tasks Accomplished:

Enhanced and updated understanding of the project's critical performance implications.

Updated resource constraints, including budget, personnel, and equipment.

Improved coordination among team members.

Enhanced communication strategies within the team.

Revised the performance-testing strategy.

Refined estimates for equipment and resources needed for conducting performance testing.

Identified incompatibilities or conflicts between the objectives of the performance-testing effort and the available equipment and resources.

Captured additional performance goals, requirements, targets, and thresholds.

Documented additional usage scenarios of particular concern.

Reported the current status of performance testing.

Coordination Required With: The entire team

5.4.4. Activity 14. Re-prioritise Tasks

Based on the test results, newly gathered information, and the availability of features and components, re-prioritize, add, or remove tasks from the performance test as necessary.

Checklist:

Questions to Ask:

Addressing Performance Concerns: What performance-testing activities will help address the currently known performance issues?

Performance Goals for the Cycle: What is the performance goal for this testing cycle?

Project Status in Relation to Goals: Where does the project stand concerning the overall performance goals?

Achievement of Performance Objectives: Has the system met all its performance objectives?

Tuning Updates: Has any tuning been completed since the last testing cycle?

Value-Adding Activities: What analysis, reports, or retesting will provide value in the next cycle?

Resource Requirements: What resources are needed for this cycle?

Time Availability: How much time is available for testing activities?

Task Duration Estimates: How long does each task take?

Critical Activities: What is the most critical activity for this cycle?

Value Provided:

Insight into how well the overall project is achieving its goals.

Information on what can be measured and reported during this cycle.

Identification of any critical issues that may have arisen from the previous iteration.

Suggestions and recommendations for other team members.

Transfer of lessons learned as they emerge from testing.

Tasks Accomplished:

Reported the current status of performance testing.

Estimated the amount of work that can be realistically achieved.

Prioritized achievable tasks.

Identified primary and alternate tasks for this cycle.

Coordination Required With:

Managers and stakeholders

Subject matter experts

Developers and administrators

Infrastructure and test environment support

Users or user representatives

6. PERFORMANCE TEST TOOLS

A range of performance testing tools is available, both open-source and commercial. While this topic is beyond the scope of this book, please feel free to contact the author for assistance in selecting the appropriate tools for your need

7. DIAGNOSTICS AND PERFORMANCE MONITORING

Ideally, the monitoring and alerting tools implemented in production   live environments should also be deployed in development, integration, and performance test environments. These tools should be utilized during performance testing to monitor their status and performance.

If you need assistance with performance monitoring, please reach out to the author

In addition to monitoring physical and virtual machine usage, application performance, middleware, and server resources (both Windows and UNIX/AIX), database monitors should be analyzed alongside transaction response times and message/transaction throughput to assess overall performance. If necessary, system administrators should be consulted regarding the use of monitoring tools to capture metrics such as CPU usage, memory, swap space, disk I/O, and other performance indicators. Various performance monitoring and data collection tools can be employed for this purpose, including but not limited to:

Unix commands and tools for performance monitoring include **"top," "iostat," "vmstat,"** and **"nmon."** On Windows, **"Perfmon"** is commonly used. For database monitoring, tools like Microsoft's **"Perfmon"** counters and Oracle's native monitoring tables are effective. Additionally, network monitoring tools and SAN/ storage monitoring solutions play a crucial role in performance analysis.

Collectd is a daemon that gathers metrics from various sources, such as the operating system, applications, log files, and external devices. It stores this information or makes it available over the network, enabling users to monitor systems, identify performance bottlenecks, and predict future system load for capacity planning. The collected data can be integrated into reporting tools to generate graphs and reports.

InfluxDB is a time-series database designed to handle large volumes of timestamped data, making it suitable for use cases like DevOps monitoring, application metrics, IoT sensor data, and real-time analytics.

Grafana is an open-source analytics and visualization suite that allows users to visualize time-series data for infrastructure and application analytics effectively.

8. TEST DATA

Performance testing relies on data from various sources, depending on the specific requirements of each test and the availability of data. A critical aspect of performance testing is that the dataset used must closely resemble 'real' or 'live' data. Consequently, performance tests require large volumes of data, ideally a complete copy of production data.

When working with sensitive production or live data, regulatory and privacy considerations may apply, necessitating the implementation of data privacy solutions that can scramble or generate suitable data. The closer the volume and structure of the data in the performance test environment are to that in production, the more accurate the performance test results will be. Testing with nearly empty databases can lead to overly optimistic results and may conceal potential database and code inefficiencies until they surface later in production.

Additionally, it is important to consider the behavior of data caches when measuring the performance of a system. At the start of a performance test, a cache can be in one of the following states:

1. Empty.
2. Pseudo-random
3. Partially randomised
4. Deterministic
5. Fully randomised

States (1) and (2): An empty or pseudo-random cache yields repeatable test results because the cache is in the same state from one test run to another. This is useful when needing to ascertain the performance behaviour of "the system" against the same dataset, when issues are found.

State (3) and (4): A partially randomised or deterministic cache contains pages left by transactions that were just executed. Such pages could be the result of a previous test run. In these cases, if the next test steps request those pages, then no disk I/O will be needed.

Therefore states (3) and (4) can bias the results away from a controlled test and a random 'live' like test, which can lead to inaccurate performance estimates.

For new systems the best testing strategy is to start with an empty cache, then make sure that all test steps access random parts of the databases. Thus ensuring that a mix of updates, writes and queries are executed which are consistent with the planned mix of activity.

Traditional Approaches to Obtaining Volume Data:

Use of Production Data: When available, utilize a copy of production data that has been sanitized to remove any personal information.

Synthetic Data Generation: If production data is not accessible, create synthetic data based on current understanding of volume and structure.

Considerations for Selecting the Test Data Approach:

Representativeness of Production Data: Production or live data is more likely to yield representative test results. However, production databases can be complex and large, posing challenges in terms of management and analysis.

Sensitive Information: Production data may contain sensitive or personal information, necessitating anonymization or adherence to specific security policies.

Simplicity of Synthetic Data: While the structure of synthetic test data is generally simpler, it may lead to discrepancies in how the production system performs during testing compared to expectations.

Availability of Similar Data Items: It can be challenging to find sufficient quantities of similar data items in production or live data for use in test scripts. As a result, additional synthetic test data might be required to facilitate comprehensive testing.

Changes in Data Structure: If new data items are being created, their structure may differ from that of migrated data. This can lead to variations in performance based on the selected data or changes in production/live performance over time as the volume of new data increases.

9. PERFORMANCE CONCLUSION

Performance testing and optimizing "the system" can be challenging. However, by utilizing the appropriate testing tools and adhering to the processes outlined in this strategy, it is possible to effectively identify bottlenecks in "the system" and manage performance testing efficiently

Failure Modes Effects and Criticality Analysis (FMECA)

11. FMECA INTRODUCTION

Implementing Failure Modes, Effects, and Criticality Analysis (FMECA)

This section outlines an approach for implementing Failure Modes, Effects, and Criticality Analysis (FMECA). It is organized into five sections:

Overview
Methodology
Using FMECA
Conclusion
Appendices

The following chapters offer an overview of FMECA analysis techniques, requirements, and guidance on effectively implementing these methods to enhance your performance testing within your organization.

12. FMECA OVERVIEW

To contextualize FMECA, it is an internationally recognized standard that identifies potential failure effects and their consequences. By ranking potential issues based on their Severity and Criticality, the FMECA process highlights areas of greatest concern in both logical and physical designs at the system, cross-system/functionality, or component level, rather than focusing solely on risks associated with individual projects.

FMECA supports various engineering activities, including:

Reliability Analyses: FMECA identifies critical areas from a logistical perspective, allowing for targeted design changes or focused non-functional testing to enhance reliability.

Performance Analysis: FMECA pinpoints significant concerns related to performance behavior, enabling targeted design modifications or non-functional testing aimed at improving performance.

Maintainability Analyses: FMECA often highlights design aspects that require scheduled maintenance activities.
Testability Analyses: FMECA includes detailed assessments of detection methods to ensure effective testing.

Safety Analyses: The results of failure mode criticality often contribute to Fault Tree Analyses for enhanced safety evaluations.

Cross-System/Functional Analyses: FMECA identifies potential impacts on existing functionalities, applications, shared systems, and components, facilitating further impact assessments where necessary.

Volumetrics: FMECA can also be expanded to include volumetric considerations associated with each application, process, or component being analyzed.

In general, FMECA requires the identification of the following essential information:

Item(s)
Function(s)
Failure(s)
Effects of Failure
Causes of Failure
Current Control(s)
Volumetrics (including workload profile, average, and peak)
Recommended Action(s)
Other Relevant Details

The procedure also incorporates a method for assessing the risks associated with the identified issues and prioritizing corrective actions accordingly.

13 FMECA METHODOLOGY

13.1. Steps

The steps for conducting a FMECA include:

1. Assemble the Team
2. Establish Ground Rules
3. Gather and Review Relevant Information
4. Identify the Item(s) or Process(es) to be Analyzed
5. Identify the Function(s), Failure(s), Effect(s), Cause(s), and Control(s) for each item or process under analysis
6. Determine the Volumetric(s) for each item or process being analyzed
7. Evaluate the Risks associated with the identified issues
8. Prioritize and Assign Actions
9. Implement Actions and Re-evaluate Risks
10. Distribute, Review, and Update the Analysis as necessary

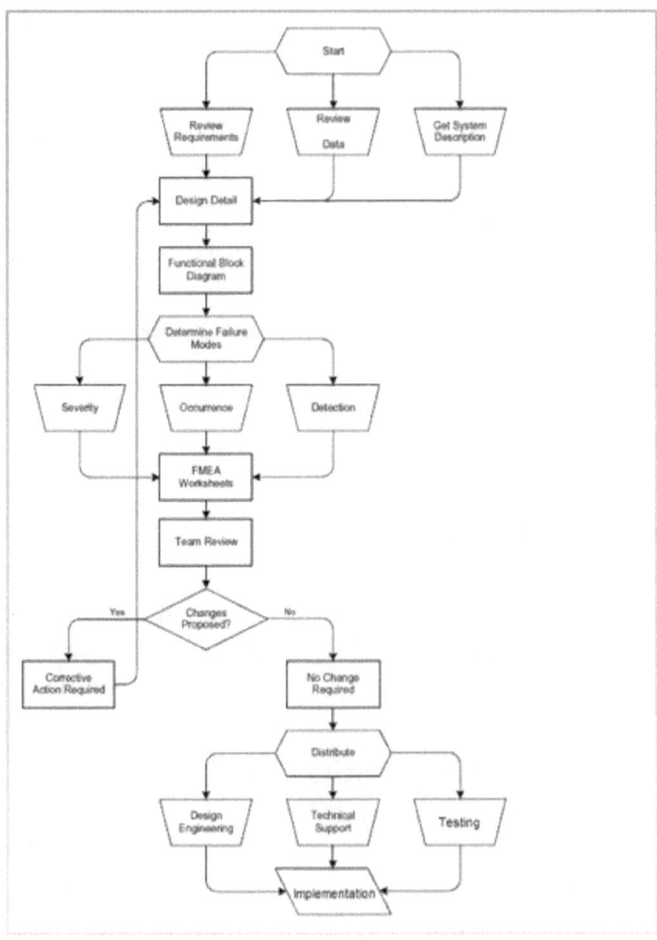

Start
Review Requirements
Review Data
Get System Description
Design Detail
Functional Block Diagram
Determine Failure Modes
Severity
Occurrence
Detection
FMEA Worksheets
Team Review
Changes Proposed?
Yes
No
Corrective Action Required
No Change Required
Distribute
Design Engineering
Technical Support
Testing
Implementation

13.2. Risk Evaluation

A typical Failure Modes and Effects Analysis (FMEA) includes a method for evaluating the risks associated with potential problems identified during the analysis. The recommended approach is to use Risk Priority Numbers (RPN), as outlined below.

To utilize the RPN method for risk assessment, the analysis team should:

Rate the Severity of each effect of failure.

Rate the Likelihood of Occurrence for each cause of failure.

Rate the Likelihood of Prior Detection for each cause of failure (i.e., the probability of detecting the issue before it affects the end user or customer).

Calculate the RPN by multiplying the three ratings: RPN = Severity x Occurrence x Detection

The RPN is employed to compare issues within the analysis and to prioritize problems for corrective action or further investigation.

14. USING FMECA

14.1. When to do a FMECA

To be effective, the purpose and scope of the FMECA must be clearly defined and implemented at the appropriate stage of the development process. If the FMECA is conducted too early, there may not be sufficient information to generate a meaningful analysis. Conversely, if it is implemented too late, any resulting design changes could incur significantly higher costs in terms of time and resources.

There are two approaches to FMECA: Functional FMECA and Component Level FMECA.

Functional FMECA

When detailed design information is not yet available, a Functional FMECA can still be performed. This approach typically involves creating a set of Functional Block Diagrams (FBDs) that identify relevant interactions and functions. A Functional FMECA can provide early insights into potential design issues. Key characteristics of a typical Functional FMECA include:

No completed designs are necessary.
High potential for influencing design decisions.
Highlights areas that require focused or targeted testing.
Provides analysis at a relatively high level.

Component Level FMECA

Component Level FMECA can be conducted later in the design process and offers a more detailed analysis from a failure perspective. Typical characteristics of a Component Level FMECA include:

Preliminary software and hardware designs are required at a minimum.

Design changes identified at this stage are likely to be costly.

Provides low-level analysis that can impact and support various subsequent analyses.

By understanding when to implement each type of FMECA, organizations can effectively manage risks and improve their design processes.

14.2. Harware FMECA

FMECA can be conducted at different stages of the development process:

Early in Development: (after design, before implementation):
In this phase, FMECA is used to assess whether the design is sufficiently robust—that is, capable of withstanding likely types of failure. If the analysis indicates weaknesses, modifications can be made to enhance the fault tolerance of the operational system.

Late in Development: (after implementation):
At this stage, FMECA evaluates the level of confidence that can be justifiably placed in the system for its operational use. This helps determine the reliability and effectiveness of the system in real-world applications.

14.3. Software FMECA

Software FMECA (SWFMECA) is an analytical technique specifically designed for software. The key distinction from traditional Hardware FMECA is the acknowledgment that software design is not assumed to be flawless; it is likely to contain systematic faults unintentionally introduced by developers. In any non-trivial software application, latent faults are almost always present, regardless of the development techniques, programming languages, or quality procedures employed. While exhaustive testing is theoretically ideal, it is often impractical, and without complete test coverage, there remains a risk that some faults will go undetected.

Assessing the likelihood and types of latent faults (failure modes) in a software design or implementation necessitates two forms of SWFMECA: one focused on the processes involved and the other on the product design itself.

Process: This aspect addresses the development and verification processes (e.g., static reviews and unit testing). It requires a thorough understanding of software development methodologies, as well as the verification and validation techniques and quality control measures used throughout the process. Knowledge of potential faults associated with specific design techniques or programming languages, along with an understanding of the fault coverage provided by chosen verification and validation methods, is essential.

Product: This component focuses on analyzing the design or implementation of the software itself.

14.4. System FMECA

System FMECA (SYFMECA) integrates SWFMECA and hardware FMECA within the Software Development Life Cycle (SDLC) framework, acknowledging the potential for both systematic and random faults. SYFMECA encompasses the entire delivered system, including both hardware and software, as well as its process history.

The process history includes the techniques employed to develop the system, as well as the methods used to verify and validate its components and the system as a whole. Metrics related to the system under analysis are collected and compared against a historical database of metrics. Statistical pattern matching is then performed to identify components with similar metric characteristics to those of the current system components, assessing whether these components were previously reported as faulty or required significant effort to maintain.

15. FMECA CONCLUSION

FMECA offers a systematic approach for identifying and assessing potential design weaknesses. When implemented effectively, FMECA serves as an impartial design review tool, highlighting areas that may require design modifications, process changes, or focused non-functional testing. Additionally, it creates a knowledge base of failure modes and corrective actions that can be invaluable for future troubleshooting efforts, as well as for Quality Assurance and Testing.

For optimal results, it is advisable to conduct a FMECA at the start of every IT project and then every three months thereafter. While FMECA can be applied at any stage of the project lifecycle, initiating the process early is preferable. Early detection of potential defects is crucial for a company to maintain control over quality and manage costs effectively.

APPENDIX A – EXAMPLE FMECA WORKSHEET

The table below is an example of a FMECA Worksheet:

Failure modes and effects analysis (FMEA)

Project:

Date:

FMECA Team:

Prepared by:

SEV = How severe is effect on the customer?
OCC = How frequent is the cause likely to occur?
DET = How probable is detection of cause?
RPN = Risk priority number in order to rank concerns; calculated as SEV x OCC x DET

Process step	Potential failure mode	Potential failure effects	S E V	Potential causes	O C C	Current process controls	D E T	R P N	Volumes (Avg & Peak)	Actions recommended	Responsibility (target date)
What is the step?	In what ways can the step go wrong?	What is the impact on the customer if the failure mode is not prevented or corrected?	10	What causes the step to go wrong? (i.e., How could the failure mode occur?)	10	What are the existing controls that either prevent the failure mode from occurring or detect it should it occur?	10	1000		What are the actions for reducing the occurrence of the cause or for improving its detection? You should provide actions on all high RPNs and on severity ratings of 9 or 10	Who is responsible for the recommended action? What date should it be completed by?
								0			

APPENDIX B – EXAMPLE RATING SCORES

The table below is an example of the FMECA Rating Scores:

RATING	DEGREE OF SEVERITY	PROBABILITY OF OCCURRENCE	Frequency (1 in …)	ABILITY TO DETECT	Detection certainty
1	Customer will not notice the adverse effect or it is insignificant	Likelihood of occurrence is remote	1,000,000	Sure that the potential failure will be found or prevented before reaching the next customer	100%
2	Customer will probably experience slight annoyance	Low failure rate with supporting documentation	20,000	Almost certain that the potential failure will be found or prevented before reaching the next customer	99%
3	Customer will experience annoyance due to the slight degradation of performance	Low failure rate without supporting documentation	5,000	Low likelihood that the potential failure will reach the next customer undetected	95
4	Customer dissatisfaction due to reduced performance	Occasional failures	2,000	Controls may detect or prevent the potential failure from reaching the next customer	90
5	Customer is made uncomfortable or their productivity is reduced by the continued degradation of the effect	Relatively moderate failure rate with supporting documentation	500	Moderate likelihood that the potential failure will reach the next customer	85
6	Warranty repair or significant manufacturing or assembly complaint	Moderate failure rate without supporting documentation	100	Controls are unlikely to detect or prevent the potential failure from reaching the next customer	80
7	High degree of customer dissatisfaction due to component failure without complete loss of function. Productivity impacted by high scrap or rework levels	Relatively high failure rate with supporting documentation	50	Poor likelihood that the potential failure will be detected or prevented before reaching the next customer	70
8	Very high degree of dissatisfaction due to the loss of function without a negative impact on safety or governmental regulations	High failure rate without supporting documentation	20	Very poor likelihood that the potential failure will be detected or prevented before reaching the next customer	60
9	Customer endangered due to the adverse effect on safe system performance with warning before failure or violation of governmental regulations	Failure is almost certain based on warranty data or significant DV testing	10	Current controls probably will not even detect the potential failure	50
10	Customer endangered due to the adverse effect on safe system performance without warning before failure or violation of governmental regulations	Assured of failure based on warranty data or significant DV testing	2	Absolute certainty that the current controls will not detect the potential failure	< 50

APPENDIX C – EXAMPLE RISK MATRIX

The table below is an example of the FMECA Risk Matrix

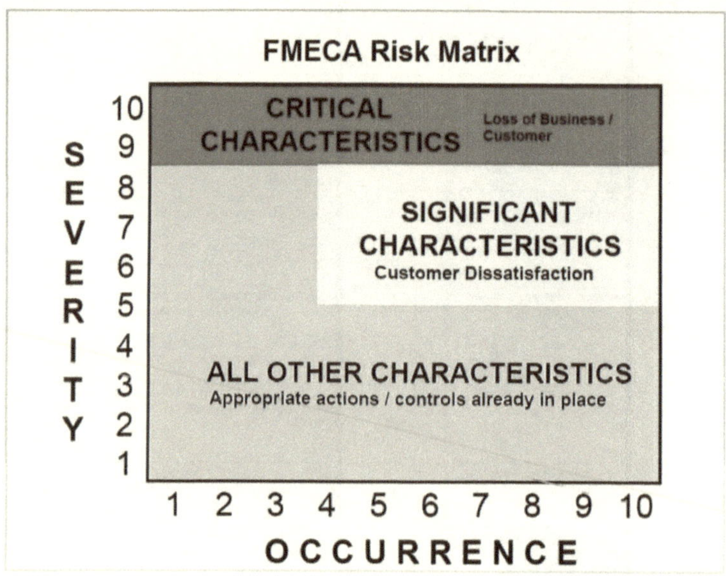